AUTHOR
BODIO, S.

CLASS
636 · 596

TITLE Aloft, meditation on pigeons and
pigeons flying

ALOFT

Books by Stephen J. Bodio

A Rage for Falcons

Good Guns

Aloft

Aloft

A Meditation on Pigeons and Pigeon-Flying

STEPHEN J. BODIO

Lyons & Burford
Publishers

Illustrations by the author

*Special thanks to Colleen Grayson,
and her computer.*

05081212

© 1990 by Stephen J. Bodio

Printed in the United States of America

10 9 8 7 6 5 4 3 2 1

Library of Congress Cataloging-in-Publication Data

Bodio, Stephen.
    Aloft : a meditation on pigeons and
pigeon-flying / Stephen J. Bodio
        p.   cm.
    ISBN 1-55821-054-7 : $15.95
    1. Homing pigeons.   2. Pigeon racing
    I. Title.
SF469.B63   1990
636.5'96—dc20   *90-5591*
                                                        CIP

FOR MY MOTHER,

who put up with pigeons when I was a child;
and for José Morales Serrano of Sevilla, Spain;
Rudy Lucero of Alamo, New Mexico;
and Shannon Hiatt of Canutillo, Texas:
my partners.

IT IS NOTORIOUS TO ALL MANKIND, WHAT VAST NUM-
bers of these Birds, in all species, have been, and
are still kept in this kingdom, not only by persons
in a lower rank of life, but even by persons of the
greatest distinction, and the first degree of quality,
who have held these birds in so great esteem, that
they have endeavored to attain at least an experi-
mental knowledge of them, purchasing, at very
great expense, as many of the distinct forms as
they could hear of, and cultivating them in their
own houses.

Moore, *Treatise on Domestic Pigeons* (1735)

CHAPTER 1

IN THE EARLY MORNING, when I fly my birds, the local wildlife has been up for hours. Towhees flirt up from the ground to the old fence and the sweet whistles of house finches rain down from above. There's a quail on a fence post and a mocker skulking away, his wings whirling like one of those mechanical windmill birds. From the pigeon loft comes the rhythmic clapping of a cock's wings as he pursues a hen to the floor, followed by his rolling courting call. I can see his stiff-tailed inflated strut before I even open the doors.

I stop to scan the sky for hawks. It is a time of pastel colors. The sun rises here long before it emerges from behind the shoulders of the Magdalena Mountains, so that it is light but without glare for at least an hour. On this winter morning there are lead-colored clouds to the west and a stiff breeze. These may be good signs. Nothing deters a falcon. But the juvenile Cooper's hawks and sharp-shins that hang around the nearby town in winter are another matter. They live off the bounty of the village, eating starlings and baby fighting chickens

1

and sparrows. Forest birds, they seem to regard the town, with its diverse plantings and narrow alleys, as an artificial woods. On still days they will venture out, sneaking from tree to tree, and I have had one dash from my isolated Siberian elm to bear away a pigeon. But their long tails and short wings—evolved to twist through tangles—are less than handy in the wind, and they stay in town.

So: over to the loft, first coffee still in hand, to throw down the outside bird door. The first two fliers hurtle through the opening, barely missing me, and flap away down wind, banging their wings like a newly mated pair. In a moment they are climbing, at first dark against the sky, then with white wingtips flashing against the blue Magdalenas. Five, six more shoot out over my shoulder, climbing after them, then all the rest in five or six coordinated bunches. Three late risers veer around me as I go to close the door. By the time I climb the ladder to my roof they are all out of sight. I turn, and turn again—and there they are, coming straight toward me from town, shooting overhead, down the wind, with a multiplied sigh of wings. They are much higher than I thought they would be, and still climbing.

As they pass again in front of the rough flank of the Magdalenas, I can see individual Catalonian tumblers falling, sideslipping, twirling, flaring in corkscrew patterns. Spanish pouters gobble air like animated balloons. Homers just stroke on forward. Yet somehow the diverse flock, flashing white and gray and brown, maintains its coherence. It is more

2

CATALONIAN TUMBLER—
gold-necked, white-tailed
black male with a frill. Notice "square" head and
wide eye-cere.

like some ghost or animated cloud than a group of
individual organisms. I can imagine a little of what
it sees with its multiple eyes—each of which has a
much wider field, forward and back, up and down,
than a human's has—the pale rectangles of the
town, the roll of dry grass and rabbitbrush to the
north, the mountain wall like a dinosaur backbone
stretching south, all passing by in a rush of wind at
something close to fifty miles an hour.

But what must they feel? The wind, sure, the
beat of wings, the rise and fall and turn and skid,
the glide and dizzying fall. My mind goes out with
my domestic sky probe and imagines a little of this.
Still, the pigeon's world view—their *umwelt* as the
German professors of animal behavior would have
it—contains much that is alien to a human accus-
tomed to living in two dimensions with a certain
narrow band of senses. Pigeons see colors, but also
see *into* the ultraviolet. They may well see bands of
ultraviolet in the sky, feel electromagnetic waves,
hear the ultrasound produced by mountains, and
navigate by all the above.

With the help of scientists, fanciers have begun

to understand the pigeon's senses. But long before they understood, they observed and worked with the birds. Pigeons have always "homed," and this characteristic, together with the bird's fecundity and genetic plasticity, earned it an early niche in man's society—perhaps an earlier one even than the chicken. Pigeons lived on farms and in towns, were eaten, played roles in sport and war and communication. It might not be too much to say that man's imagination first navigated the air on the wings of a Middle Eastern rock dove.

It still does. I know that as the line of dawn advances around the world, other fanciers on other rooftops have sent out their sky probes. In Diyarbakir, Turkey, nine hours before I rose, a townsman sent aloft two Syrian dewlaps, handsome horse-headed birds almost as big as peregrine falcons, coal black with white wingtips and forehead blazes. After watching them fly wing to wing five thousand feet above for a half-hour, he tosses a fat white bird out onto the roof. Instantly the two dewlaps fold and fall head-first, cleaving the air like hawks. They are "divers," birds bred for falconlike stoops, and they accelerate toward the loft without a flutter, only corkscrewing a little from the resistance of the solid air on their half-folded wings. Ten feet above the ground, just as it seems they must smash against the pavement, they unfurl, brake with heavy flaps, and flutter through the open doors of their master's "cupboard loft," where they begin to peck up their morning ration.

A little later, in a village near Seville, an old fan-

4

cier tests the wind with his hand on the loft door. He is one of the last breeders of the ancient, and at first sight grotesque, varieties of Spanish "thief" pouters. These pigeons have immense crops they fill with air, often becoming so large and loose that they sag like flabby beer bellies. According to their breed, they may also have parrot bills, "ram heads," wattles on nose and chin, and eyes circled with bare skin. They are direct descendants of birds brought by the Moors and have flown for centuries to steal or seduce females from rival lofts in a sport so formal and organized the Spanish government regulates it.

After the Spanish civil war the old breeds nearly disappeared. For a while the government actually banned them, even as modern fanciers crossed them with speedier, more streamlined Belgian homers. But a few traditionalists, this old man among them, knew that the pure ancient breeds (one of the more recent was developed by a Franciscan friar in 1799) had more instinct for seduction, whatever their aerodynamics.

Which are none too great. The old man flies

MARCHENERO—
flying like a potbellied owl.

5

Marcheneros, one of the most persistent yet probably the clumsiest of all the *Buchonas Espanolas*. Not only does it carry a round inflated crop rather larger than a grapefruit, it also has a convex back like a lobster and a short tail that it carries splayed against the air. As one Spanish writer says, it can easily become "a toy for the wind," especially in the strong winds north of the Straits of Gibraltar.

But this morning the winds have died down, and the old man releases his little flock. The birds whir up like helicopters and swing above the buildings into the sun with a sort of heavy joy. Their ridiculous "tile tails" are spread, breaking the wind just enough to give their flight an odd buoyancy. They look like nothing else on earth.

Fifteen hundred miles to the northeast, on a geometrically ordered plot of land outside Antwerp, stands a line of whitewashed brick buildings with skylights and red-tiled roofs. Each is bigger than the house of the Spanish or New Mexican fanciers (the Turkish flier lives in an apartment). The Belgian professional paces the walk under the windows, checking his Patek Phillipe watch, looking over the tops of the trees. It is past the formal racing season, but his birds train like Olympic athletes through the winter. Right now his young birds are out on a twenty-kilometer toss. He turns again on his heel, unclasps his hands from behind his back, tugs his tie, then smiles. Low in over the trees, his "small" flock of yearling fliers—about sixty birds, culled by nature and human calculation from an initial year's hatch of two hundred—is braking and jostling for space to fly in through its home-loft doors. The wing song changes pitch from the whisper of speeding flight to a clatter and whistle as the birds peel off from the circling main flock. The Belgian takes careful mental note of a few favorites, all among the first birds to detach themselves and enter the buildings. Unlike American fanciers, most Belgians do not encourage their birds to land on the roof and waddle in through pigeon doors, but rather to fly in straight from the sky. In the hypercompetitive world of Belgian racing, literal splitseconds count.

And as dawn's edge moves westward round the waking planet, fanciers continue to rise and send up their sky probes. Competitive flock flyers in Barcelona and Brooklyn maneuver their aerial armies over the sleeping cities, directing their flocks with flags, trying to merge the hundred-eyed flock mind with a competitor's kit, then bring it "crashing" in to the home loft. The breeds are different—fisheyed, crested, tiger-marked flights in Brooklyn; multicolored Catalonian tumblers in northern Spain. But the game is the same. In Hawaii, lateseason racers fly low above the heaving seas between the islands, following invisible skymarks, out of sight of land. In Hong Kong, a wealthy Chinese businessman attaches multiple lacquered flutes carved from bamboo and hardwoods to the tails of a little group of "bloody-red blue-eyes" and beak-crested pigeons. Some of the flutes seem impossibly intricate, with two large chambers and eighteen small whistles, but the heaviest weighs only three quarters of an ounce. All were made before the turn of the century. Most of the few present-day owners of such whistles keep them in locked cabinets, or maybe send them up for one exhibition flight a year with modern homers. But this last traditionalist prefers the old mainland breeds and flies them, weather permitting, every day.

All over the world in city and country, rich men, poor men, young men and old, are exploring the dawn as they have done for at least six thousand years. The pigeons are flying.

CHAPTER 2

 "HOW WOULD YOU LIKE TO have some pigeons with feathers on their feet?" asked my father. I was eight. My father, whose enthusiasm for hunting, bird-watching, and natural history is responsible for my own, had just returned from the wedding of one of our innumerable relatives. As a respite from the usual blather at such functions, he had fallen into conversation about birds with my great-uncle John Derosier. "Uncle Joe" (as he was known to distinguish him from his brother-in-law Uncle John McCabe) was a semi-retired businessman whose life's passion was birds. Anything with feathers caught his eye. He had bird feeders and subscribed to something called *Game Breeder's Gazette*. But his real love was the domestic pigeon.

I couldn't quite picture such an animal. Feathers on the feet? Did they walk on them? But I was interested. I already had a virtual menagerie of toads, frogs, and snakes and had recently and reluctantly set free a blue jay that had become notorious for stealing frying bacon from the pan. Maybe my par-

9

ents felt that more controllable, or less slimy, pets would be an improvement. My father built a four-foot cube on legs with a screen front and a nestbox and then drove up to Boston's North Shore to return with a pair of saddle-marked muffed tumblers.

Maybe I have romanticized them over time, but it's hard to think of a more attractive bird than a marked tumbler. I pressed my eyes against the air

MUFFLED TUMBLER—
my first pigeons.

holes punched into the corrugated cardboard box to see two creatures that, to my innocent eyes, didn't look like pigeons at all. They were smaller than the Boston Common birds that were the only ones I had seen up close, and had short, whitish beaks and high foreheads. Their legs were swaddled from thigh to ankle with a profusion of white feathers that got longer as they went lower on the leg, so that each bird marched on clown's feet; the longest feathers, which made their feet invisible unless you turned the bird upside down, were four inches long. Their eyes were those of cartoon characters, a startling silvery white with black pupils. And the color! Each bird had white wings and leg muffs, and a complicated blaze and whisker marking in white on its face. But the rest was a glistening iridescent black revealing purple and green ripples as the bird moved.

I had never been so taken with any living creature. At first I hardly dared touch them, and instead spent all my time quietly staring into the hutchlike building. I watched them eat and strut and throw themselves around with abandoned spasms in their bath pan. Just as happily, I watched them sleep for hours at a time and sit on their new eggs.

What I didn't know was that my father had been bitten by the bug. Probably he had been going up to Uncle Joe's on race day—I don't remember. What I do remember is that soon a much larger building began to take shape beside the hutch.

To this day I don't know whether my father was kidding himself or, in the way of the fifties, placating my mother when he told her he was building a garden shed with "a little room up under the roof" for pigeons. But when it assumed eight-by-eight dimensions, with a larger "fly pen" extending all the way to the tumbler hutch, he could no longer conceal his purpose.

That was 1958, the beginning of a ten-year period in my father's life when he devoted more to pigeons than to any other objective I could see—one that would culminate in his dominance of the six-hundred-mile Sandusky, Ohio to Boston race. It was also, I now think, a formative period for me, one that consolidated the naturalistic and sporting passions for falcons, pigeons, coursing dogs, span-

11

iels, reptiles, and odd insects that have made my life, well, not rich exactly, but at least never boring. It was my introduction to the life of the enthusiast.

Which is all hindsight. At the time, all I knew was that pigeons suddenly revealed to me a large group of grown men who cared as much about birds as I did. First and foremost there was Uncle Joe, with his long pale face and gentle scholar's voice punctuated at precise intervals with what I thought was a polite cough. Next was his friend, the terrifying Max Koenig. Maxie was a thin old German with the manner of a cavalry officer and a thick accent who did not suffer fools, period. He had a flower garden that grew in regimented weedless rows, and pigeons—mostly small tight-feathered "grizzles"—that all but stood at attention when he snapped his fingers and muttered "Peanuts, pigeons, peanuts." He powdered his loft floors with lime twice a day and had a disconcerting habit, when you visited his loft, of picking up each dropping as it was deposited. I doubt that, except at night, one ever lasted long enough to dry out. But Max was a lot more than fussy. He won races. Uncle Joe's sloppiness appalled him, though one gradually got the idea that their arguments had been perfected over forty years.

"John, John, you're too sentimental. Kill that one, and that one, and that big hen. How are you ever going to win feeding all these *losers*?"

"Oh, I don't know, Max. Her mother was good. Give her another year. She doesn't eat that much."

"She's six years old already."

12

I was afraid of Max and considered him rather brutal. Then one day I held a "worthless" hen for an hour while he lanced a boil on its wing, cleaned it out with swabs and antiseptic, and bound the wing to her body, crooning to her all the while. His thin hands moved as gently and as deftly as a surgeon's. "Now, sonny, don't you let her fly at all for a month. Or she'll be *no damn good.*" I came away with perhaps a little more intuitive understanding of the perfectionist animal breeder, a man whose ideal will not yield to the temptation of sentimentality. But again, this is hindsight speaking. I still went in fear of Max.

In time, as the "garden shed" filled with gifts (the fancy is contagious; fanciers distribute extra birds with the abandon of a cold sufferer distributing germs) and five-dollar "squeakers," I met more fanciers, some of them local. There was Dr. Hubbard, a remote ancient of purest Yankee stock who wore gold-rimmed specs and dressed in three-piece suits of heavy wool at conclaves where others wore dirty T-shirts. He had a walled house and a fading obstetrical practice in Cambridge and an estate on the South Shore where he raised horses, bull terriers, game fowl, and racing pigeons. More accessible were Fran Poleski, a disabled World War II vet whose wheelchair didn't seem to slow him down when in pursuit of a bird, and the Nessralla brothers, whose farm in Brockton housed hundreds of pigeons and chickens.

But my best friend among them all soon became Andy Better. Old Andy was a huge-bellied retired something or other who lived in some elegance in the never-finished foundation of his house with his wife, a former dancer. Beside the foundation stood—towered—a nineteenth century barn containing his pigeon loft and an immense plastic goat's head bearing the enigmatic legend "The Pickwick Bock."

Andy was as uninhibited as a child, and ten times as loud. He would emerge slowly from his aged Ford and stand beside it in the driveway, bellowing *"WHERE'S JOE? WHERE'S STEVE?"* His loudness always embarrassed my mother, who would beg my father to go outside and quiet him down. And, perhaps because she was shy of him, she would ask me to do the same if my father wasn't home. Which in turn led to many expeditions and meetings with most of the pigeon fanciers in a fifty-mile radius. To send us both away was the only way to get rid of Andy.

Andy treated pigeon fanciers from eight to eighty with the same respect and the same *ex cathedra* pronouncements. I can see him to this day, pushing back his baseball cap in order to see as he holds one of my favorite birds up against the light. He touches an enormous index finger to the bird's rather square skull and bellows, *"THIS BIRD'LL NEVER BE ANY GOOD. IT HAS A DEPRESSED BRAIN!"*

In spite of which pronouncement, he was as good a friend as this rather reclusive child ever had. Over the next few years I was to visit many lofts and meet many fanciers. As my father joined forces with John Morse, a local banker, to import fine Belgian and French racers that they blended with birds from the winning strain of boozy old Tim O'Connell of Boston to build a great long-distance family, I was to see many birds of quality undreamed of in 1958. But I don't think I ever had so much fun as on those expeditions with Andy.

I particularly remember one trip, in 1959. It was perhaps the only time I've seen a town of pigeon fanciers, though I'm sure that I could find a similar gathering in, say, Barcelona or Turkey. Still, I suspect that "Pigeon Village" is unique in the New World.

It was a rainy morning in June when Andy arrived. "I've been telling you about Pigeon Village." He hadn't, though what you replied to Andy made little difference. "We'll go down there today. I don't know if they're racing or not. Doesn't matter. Matthews'll be there—he's moved up for the summer." I just smiled and nodded. Andy tended to reduce me to silence.

Our destination was the crumbling old whaling port of New Bedford. These days commuter sprawl has turned the cranberry county towns into suburban bedrooms for Boston and the high-tech complexes, but in those days, less than thirty years ago, New Bedford seemed remote and exotic, a Portuguese island an hour away through a swamp-Yankee sea. When we reached the city, Andy navigated through a maze of narrow streets and brick houses and finally climbed a steep hill. As the hill flattened, the houses fell away. The vacant space at the top was not beautiful. It resembled any open urban space not formally designated a park, full of ragweed and broken bottles. But we were above the roofs of the surrounding houses, and the skyline, even under steady drizzle, was impressive.

At the far side of the lot stood perhaps twenty buildings, tall narrow structures bristling with flags and platforms. A group of dark-haired men crowded around one of them. As we watched, a homer flew in over our heads on a low trajectory, skidded a little on its curve, and pitched on one of the roofs. The second it folded its wings, the nearest man tossed a white pigeon toward the same roof. It climbed with a frantic flapping of stumpy wings, barely able to span the ten-foot gap even with the help of its owner's throw. It landed, and without pausing, scrambled through the pigeon doors with so much impetus that I could hear the clack of the swinging one-way wires from fifty feet away. The other pigeon followed, sheeplike, only to balk at the doorstep. But before it could change its mind the owner swung up what looked like a tennis racket with a ten-foot handle and pushed the bird in. Several of the men yelled and hooted while one seemed to be cursing in another language.

I had never seen anything like it. Our own races were formal affairs, bound by rules and traditions that seemed as rigid as law. After a formal survey of an individual loft's distance from each race release point—eight, one hundred, and then in increments of one hundred up to six hundred miles from Boston—each bird flew to its own loft where the exact second of its arrival was registered by an expensive sealed Belgian clock in order to compute its speed in yards per minute. You didn't know how well you had done until the clocks were opened and the results revealed at the club after your birds were in. All of which was fascinating, but maybe just a little bit abstract for a child. This looked like more fun. "How long is the race, Andy?"

He grinned. "About four miles."

I didn't believe it. Our training tosses were longer than that—I took young birds farther than that on my bicycle. "It's not as easy as you think. You see that church tower?" He pointed to a cathedral on the skyline. "One of these guys goes over there and releases the birds, two by two. They don't time 'em exactly . . . just see which one comes in first. But if the bird does more than one circle . . ." He drew his finger across his throat making a gargling sound. "And—you see how the ground goes down between us and the church?—if the bird dips down instead of flying straight across from there to here—if it follows the contour—SOUP TIME!"

His last bellow caught the attention of one of the racers, who detached himself from the group and hurried over to shake Andy's hand. He was about sixty and wore a crewneck sweater and tweed cap. He had a gray moustache and skin the color of walnut stain. "Shake hands with Mr. Matthews. He's the only one a' these Portuguese who flies long-

17

distance racers too. He has a loft and a racing house just down the hill." Matthews smiled and half-nodded, half-bowed in my direction.

"These boys think the long races are—how do you say?—too much chance." He had a pronounced accent despite his English-sounding name. "They think you know what you got when you can see the whole flight. Me, I like the long races. I think they're harder. I built myself a house for the races so my wife don't hafta put up with the birds. I just moved up for the season. Come on down and I'll give ya a cup of coffee."

But first Andy wanted to show me the village lofts. This presented a problem. The fliers were perfectly willing to tell us how they worked the birds. But they absolutely refused to show us the insides of their lofts. Their lower windows were covered with plywood, and almost every loft had a dog, a doberman or German shepherd, chained under the steps. Matthews beckoned us aside. "Don't mind the boys. But they won't show you the birds now. They're breeding. They're afraid you'll steal their breeding secrets. Or maybe that you'll tell their friends."

What could we do? We followed him to his "racing house," a snug one-room shed with chintz curtains, a hot plate, a daybed, and pictures of pigeons. I drank coffee and felt very grownup while Andy rambled on about my prowess. We ended up going out to his lofts. Matthews suddenly put me on the spot. "Okay: Andy says you're so good; pick me my best young ones." For

18

the next hour I caught birds from the air and cornered them, knowing that this was in some way a test. If a bird escaped me twice I let it alone for a while, knowing that panic was contagious. I shifted birds between my hands to calm them down, held their heads between thumb and finger to examine eye color, and fanned wings, looking for strength, breadth, solidity. I resolutely rejected anything with a depressed brain, even if its color was unbearably attractive. At the end of the time I had six birds in a crate. "These six."

"Okay kid, they're yours."

I was speechless. No one had ever rewarded my knowledge with its own fruits. The rest of the visit passed in a daze. Matthews discussed long-distance conditioning with Andy, solved the mystery of what the fancier was doing throwing the white bird at the roof ahead of his racer (it was a "dropper," a white show bird of the owl breed with its wings clipped, trained above all to trap swiftly and draw the racer in like a Judas goat leading lambs to slaughter), and complained that his wife didn't like him living four months of the year in a shack be-

AFRICAN OWL.
This show breed cannot successfully feed its own young. White ones, like this specimen, are used as "droppers" for racing homers.

19

side his birds. ("But what can she do? I'm *retired*.")
All I could think about was my new birds.

When I arrived home my father was not as impressed. He had been linebreeding—breeding parent to offspring: mother to son, father to daughter—for a couple of years to fix the characteristics he liked and wasn't too keen on any wildcard new blood. But, perhaps sensing my pride, he only muttered, "Who ever heard of a Portagee named Matthews?"

They were pretty ordinary birds, I guess: two were lost, and only one ever showed "in the numbers." But my seriousness about them was obvious even to my meticulous and driven father, and he relented from his pursuit of excellence long enough to build me a small loft of my own and to change our loft's official listing from "Bodio" to "Bodio and Son."

CHAPTER 3

 IN ANY LITTLE VILLAGE IN the Middle East you can still see towers of dried mud pierced with hundreds of holes, ancient pigeon slums that may predate the actual villages; their design, at least, is supposed to go back five thousand years. The feral mongrel types that inhabit these primitive dovecotes are neither pets nor sporting animals. They may be eaten, but their primary function is to produce fertilizer, which, if you have ever seen an old pigeon roost, you will know that they do very well. Though modern urban residents may recoil at the idea of supposedly disease-ridden pigeon droppings, you don't have to be an Egyptian peasant to use them. My paternal grandfather, an immigrant from the Italian Alps, was a passionate gardener. Twice a year he would collect the trash cans of nitrogen-rich pigeon dung that we stored up for him and spread them in his backyard to age. After a year—fresh pigeon manure will burn plants—he would apply it to his half-acre vegetable garden, on his flowers, and under his grapevines—all this, incidentally, in an inner sub-

urb of Boston! *I'm* not sure that pigeon manure was the deciding factor in the size and flavor of his crops, but he was.

Still, the oldest true breeds of pigeon are not "utility" types, but fliers, birds kept for pleasure and sport. (Is it any accident that the oldest dog breeds are for hunting and ornament? Nor are the oldest horse breeds draft horses.) The conventional

ROCK DOVE—
ancestor of them all.

view is that these were military messenger birds, but this is at best only partly true. The Arab civilization was the first culture we have record of that kept recognizable breeds of pigeon; many of their favorites survive in Spain today, and all the present-day Islamic cultures have preserved fine and venerable flying breeds. But most of these are bred for city-roof competition flying or the sport of "stealing" one's competitor's birds, not homing.

One ancient Arab breed did resemble the birds redundantly called "Syrian Bagdads" today. The Bagdad is a primitive homing pigeon—large, long-necked, and aggressive—that sports a mass of rough tissue, the wattle, on the bill, as well as a wide ring of fleshy bare skin, the eye cere, around each eye. Modern fanciers testing the breed have found that it can return from so-called short distances, under one hundred miles. In an era of slow transportation and difficult communication, such skills could seem miraculous. But these birds look a little old-fashioned today compared to the high-tech Belgian racing homer that appeared amidst the upheavals of nineteenth-century Europe. The voyageur or Antwerp* gradually replaced the older breeds, mostly because it was considered of dubious value if it couldn't return six hundred miles in a *day*.

Our world and the homing pigeon were born at the same time, in the turmoil of the Industrial Revolution, in the wars and uprootings that from the late 1700s onward transformed the stable old kingdoms into modern nation-states. The flying competitors of pub and village had always carried letters. Now they became a state-of-the-art communications tool for the expanding armies. War was not the only evolutionary pressure upon the dragon and the horseman, the cumulet and the smerle. Most breeders were still sportsmen. But as

---

*Names! Never call a homer a "carrier." The carrier is a show breed bred down directly from the Bagdad, with wattles the size of a walnut and eye ceres like fleshy fifty-cent pieces; old ones can't see well enough to fly around the loft, never mind home, though the young ones can be surprisingly efficient. The Bagdad line entered the homer mix through English sporting and post pigeons called "horsemen" and "dragons" or "dragoons," themselves working descendants of birds brought back from wars and trade with Spain and the Holy Land. Spain also has a horseman, or caballero, and had many very Arabic Bagdad-type homing breeds until the twentieth century brought the Belgian voyageur.

a new social mobility brought together gene pools that had been isolated for centuries in back-country villages, fusing their virtues and canceling out their vices, farsighted commanders began to use the best of these new crossbreeds as avian radios. Pigeons became a serious modern instrument of war at about the time of the siege of Paris, and lasted until World War II, becoming obsolete even as their efficiency topped out.

It is probably no accident that the preeminent crosses were made in Belgium, always one of Europe's prime battlegrounds. But the English, now riding the crest of imperial power, imported each new wave of homing birds, and not just for military purposes. From the laborer in his pub to the lord of the manor, the Englishman has always been a sportsman and a gambler.

Not all fanciers were working class, nor city men: Charles Darwin, whose observations of domestic breeds and their breeders gave him a framework for the theory of evolution, was neither. Sir John Sebright, the falconer who could kill a partridge with a sparrow hawk five days after he trapped the hawk, "inventor" of the Sebright bantam and the fancy pigeon breed called the pygmy pouter, was a countryman. Still, it was in cities that the competitive pigeon became the bird of choice. England's fanciers seemed more interested in individual competitors than in the sky-wars of the Continentals or the seductions of southern Spain. They flew dragoons—birds that probably originated in a cross of Bagdad types with tumblers—against each other or against the clock, sometimes for heavy wagers. A typical match would begin with a coach leaving an inn with a dragoon, and the coachman charged to release the bird at a predetermined spot. The patrons would place bets on how long it would take the bird to fly back. It is safe to assume the sportsmen consumed more ale on the horses' journey out than during the bird's swift return.

By the 1860s the sons of these alehouse hearties were importing the swifter and more reliable Belgian homer in numbers. It soon became the most popular breed in Great Britain and perhaps the world. Immigrants soon brought them to the United States. By 1901, Ernest Thompson Seton would include a sentimental but accurate account of contemporary pigeon racing, "Arnaux," in his *Animal Heroes*—a tale, incidentally, that I read aloud to my father on one of our trips to Uncle Joe's, choking up at the death of the brave racer.

In England the homer became even more popular, its fame perhaps enhanced by such well-publicized World War I messenger birds as Cher Ami, who rescued the "Lost Battalion" despite having a

RACING HOMER—
an athletic frame, no particular color.

25

leg shot off. (Though English, his stuffed body still resides in the Smithsonian.) Even today, racing homers are so ubiquitous in English culture that one of Andy Capp's identifying props, as clear a part of pub culture as his pint or snooker cue, is his basket of pigeons. Nor are homers confined to the lower classes—Queen Elizabeth has her own Royal Lofts.

Although there are country fanciers, and wealthy ones, in the United States, the heart of racing has always been among urban descendants of European immigrants, if for no other reason than you need a cluster of centrally located lofts for competition. And it was in such a club that my next level of pigeon education began.

The first thing you must understand about a long-distance pigeon race is that most of it is *invisible*. Can you link this to mysterious senses? Is this true of any other sport? Before the sudden appearance of the bird on the landing board—or, if you are very observant, in the sky—you see nothing. The bird performs its mysterious art over a course of from eight to six-hundred-odd miles. All you do is ship and receive.

In contrast with the endless waiting of the race day, when you sit alone and imagine what your bird is seeing, shipping is a bustling, social, human activity. In the fifties, my father belonged to the Dorchester Homing Pigeon Club, which met in and shipped from a garage in a blue-collar part of

Milton, Massachusetts. The little room was a slightly intimidating but still magical place for a child: hot and stuffy in the summer dusk, redolent of beer and Camels, Parodi cigars and cedar shavings and the pleasant dusty scent of pigeon feathers. Each fancier brought his baskets, of wood doweling or wicker, filled with shifting masses of birds that milled and fought and uttered rolling coos as they pecked at their neighbors. He would take out his birds one by one, holding each aloft to murmured approval or friendly jeers as the secretary recorded its permanent band number. He would then extend the bird's other foot toward a machine like a metal spider that would spread its claws to snap a numbered rubber ring, the countermark, onto the bare leg. The owner then handed the bird over to be packed, with hundreds of others, into the transport crates that would be loaded in turn onto a truck with birds from the other Boston clubs and driven to locations from Gardiner, Massachusetts (eighty miles) to Sandusky, Ohio (six hundred miles).

Now comes the technical and abstract part, frustrating to me as a child, but necessary in order to understand this strangest of all kinds of racing. After the birds are safely packed away, every racer sets his clock—an expensive six- or ten-inch-square box of wood or metal imported from Germany or Belgium—and starts it. The club officials wire the clocks shut and secure the wires with soft lead seals. On the next morning each racer will check his clock against the master clock of the "Concourse," the umbrella organization of all the clubs included in the race, to insure that every clock is running at the same speed and that no one has an accidental advantage.

In the top of each clock is a hole big enough to admit a capsule about the size of the last joint of your index finger. Below it revolves a wheel edged with receptacles for two dozen or so of these capsules. As your racers return you will catch them, remove their rubber countermarks, put each countermark into a capsule, drop the capsule into the clock, and turn a large key stuck into the top, "punching it in" with an audible clunk. The exact second that the bird arrives is then recorded on a roll of paper beneath one of the clock's windows, enabling the race authorities to compute the bird's speed in yards per minute. As your exact distance from the release point (in yards) has already been plotted by a committee of surveyors using geographical quads, the fastest bird—rather than the first one home—wins, a necessity in the only race where every contestant "runs" a slightly different course.

Two years ago, with the idea of this book taking ghostly shape in my mind like a slowly developing photograph, I visited a racing club in my father's Concourse for the first time in twenty-eight years. Though it was located thirty miles from my childhood Friday-night haunt, very little had changed. There were old Italians and cocky young gamblers, the smell of cigars and Budweiser in the summer dusk, the r-less Boston accent ("Your old man used ta fly with Dawchesta?") both strange and familiar to someone who had spent a decade in the West. The only differences I could see were longer hair, fewer unfiltered cigarettes, more moustaches, LED displays on the clocks, and talk of computer software for breeding programs. The metal spider that placed the countermarks on the birds' legs was probably in use in 1960. And I could still smell the familiar stench of Parodi, my grandfather's favorite cigar.

No fog of abstraction surrounds the actual race. The waiting is as real as hunger. From the time I was nine until I was about fourteen, I spent more Saturdays (or Sundays, if the race covered more than four hundred miles) waiting for pigeons than in almost any other activity. Since release was at dawn, I didn't have to be out there *too* early. But, however I started the day, I'd have to be sitting in my chair facing the loft at least an hour before any birds were due. If the weather was bad on Sunday, the race "bumped" to Monday, always a source of distress to my mother. My father's fierce Italian mother, who did not quite understand homing, would whisper to her that she should just "open up the coop and let them all go!"

I don't want to make it sound like a chore; it wasn't, at least until adolescence's restlessness made everything a chore. I always had an appetite for birds—all birds and any birds. I would lie on my back on the chaise lounge staring straight up into the blue until my eyes filled with transparent

29

drifting flecks. I saw my first hawks then, soaring buteos, mostly redtails, drifting in lazy circles. Sometimes they were so high up that at first I wasn't sure whether they were birds or insects or just more "floaters." On days of changing weather, at least half the time in New England, gulls would meander across the sky in twos and threes, flapping their thin crooked wings shallowly, as though they hurt. Swallows played in the middle levels, dipping and swerving and diving like miniature falcons, hunting insects. Parties of chimney swifts screamed around on invisible race tracks, chittering, chasing, buzzing their stiff sickle wings. They seemed jet-propelled, as though their flapping had nothing to do with their skidding rush. Sometimes a pair of crows would climb toward the serenely revolving hawk, squawking defiance, or a robin bounce down to the lawn, or a golden oriole chase from the tall willow to harass the crows, or a blue jay alight (that *was* a jay, wasn't it?) on the roof of the loft to look around and then hurry furtively back to the woods behind.

And while I was watching the show, the pigeons would slip in. If I were completely attentive—usually I wasn't—I'd see the bird in the air. It would come in low over the roof, flapping hard, rocking a little in the air, then braking and flaring just above the loft's roof. If a bird came in this way you didn't have to coax it; it would hustle down the slant of the roof and thrust itself through the trap entrance with an audible thud. But if the bird—or birds, for the low fliers were usually alone but the high ones often in company—came in high, it would circle maddeningly, then maybe alight on the house before it flew to the loft, prance around on the loft roof, hang up on the landing board to stare through the trap . . .

Meanwhile I'd be going crazy. The jolt of adrenalin when the bird first appeared was like buck fever, that rush of trembling when a hunter sees his quarry in his sights. And now the silly thing is just sitting there, when you know that races are won and lost by seconds. If my father was home and in charge it wasn't quite as bad; he'd rattle the feed can, curse under his breath, mutter "come on, you bugger . . ." Still, if he was there it was *his* problem. But if I was there alone I felt the weight of responsibility on my shoulders. I'd rattle the feed can, sure; I'd also whistle, walk forward, freeze if the bird raised its head to stare at me, pray, and almost cry *COME ON!*

Of course, finally the bird would drop, to be arrested in its forward movement by a lock on the swinging "bob" wires. I'd reach up to where its legs were exposed, pull the countermark, fumble it into the capsule, pop it into the clock, and turn the handle. The solid *clunk* as the mechanism recorded the time let me start breathing again. I'd reach up and unlock the bobs, the pigeon would fly in to mate or squabs or feed, and I'd return to the lawn chair. The rest of the birds—we usually only clocked three or four, except for special races— would be more fun, now that the pressure was off.

This was only a typical race day. Bad weather

that began after the release could make the whole wait even more excruciating and my father so short-tempered that nobody would dare speak to him. Sometimes there were inexplicable "busts," when, despite perfect weather and good winds, nobody's birds would come in. Maybe two or three days later a few, often not the best or most proven birds, would straggle home, much the worse for wear. If the winds were wrong on a long race, like my father's favorite six-hundred-miler, birds might come in at dusk or at dawn the next day. He eventually rigged a light to spot the landing board for these twilight travelers.

Or birds might come in torn by hawks, cut by wire, blackened with oil. Or a bird lost on a race three weeks previously might come in during another race. (I once made the mistake of clocking such a bird; from then on I made sure I knew exactly who was flying.)

I think that the uncertainties of the race irritated my father, a competitive sportsman, who liked to eliminate as much chance as possible from his calculations. But they drew me. My father, I think, dreamed of training and condition, breeding and discipline; my imagination followed the birds through the skies, pushing through weather, scanning for hawks, seeing cities from above . . . and *what*? What *else*? How did they know where to go? I didn't really care about the end of the race that much—I don't think I ever went to the club with my father to get the race results. I preferred daydreaming about the birds, or doing training tosses up to five or six miles on my bicycle. Then I could conduct my own races, remove my basket from the handlebars, face it away from oncoming cars and overhead wires, drop the front and liberate the flock in a blur and crash of blue and brown and white feathers. They'd leave the basket too fast for my eyes to follow, then curve back over the trees. I'd watch the many-eyed organism circle four or five times to get its bearing, then swing away in a straight course to the east. Or I'd single-toss, taking a nervous pigeon from the basket as it grunted in protest, holding it a minute to calm it, then bowling it upward. I remember thinking how much more fun it was to throw a bird than a ball, a living object that defied gravity and entropy, climbing instead of sinking. Single birds would circle too, but here you could begin to discern individual differences. Some would take a firm line after two or three passes; others would seem hesitant and uncertain. But one thing was sure; when I got home, they would all be waiting.

Because the race is invisible, fanciers have always been prone to improve their luck by all kinds of harmless voodoo; I'm not sure that computer programs aren't just a high-tech version of this. In other animal sports you train the body and habits rather than a sense that resides behind a wall that we cannot penetrate. You can condition pigeons but if they don't have "it" then they still won't win. What you can do is breed for "it," using signs and portents as much as charts of parents' race re-

33

sults—for every fancier knows that two mediocre birds can produce entire lines of champions, while two winners might breed nothing but trash. For many years a large minority of fanciers, including some consistent winners, have touted "eye sign." Believers examine their birds' eyes under brightly lit magnifying glasses and read everything from future performance to likely matings in the vagaries of color, texture, and structure of the iris. They speak of "circles of correlation," of "beads," of "gravel," the mysterious violet color that signifies excellence . . . all as exciting as any esoteric cult.

There are other physical attributes that some fanciers swear by, but none can guarantee success or even predict it reliably. Moderation in size and shape usually works better than extremes—there have been very large and very small champions, but not many. Most good birds feel like a wedge between your hands, with broad shoulders and full breasts tapering back toward a slim tail section. Some would go further. Joseph Rotondo, a successful racer who wrote the encyclopedic *Rotondo on Racing Pigeons*, filled eight double-column pages with detailed descriptions of keels and vent bones, wing shapes, "open" throats, and every other observable detail, delineating differences between short-distance "sprinters" and long-haul "routers." Some of his arguments, especially about wing shape, make sense; still, I have seen some off-types that flew very well. Besides, fads affect animal breeders, sometimes more than they realize. I can see a distinct difference in the average racing homer of today and the average thirty years ago—

today's birds are smaller, trimmer, less wattled, and have, to me at least, less individual character. But would I have noticed the change if I had kept up in racing homers?

Active practices are meant to increase motivation, which *does* work. They range from the simple—birds may home faster when feeding medium-sized young, or if they are ready to mate, or if (they say) you can fool them into thinking their eggs are about to hatch by putting a fly into a glass egg and placing it under the sitters—to the strenuous. Most strenuous of all is "widowhood," a kind of systematic sex-starving that requires a whole extra loft for the participating cocks. Widowhood is big in Belgium and I know successful fanciers that practice it here. I think it's too much like work, the kind of thing that happens when sport and play turn into serious competition. Until recently, though, nobody really knew anything about *homing*.

Since the real advent of the homing bird coincided with the rise of applied science in the 1800s, there has never been a shortage of theories about homing. Most nineteenth-century discussion centers on whether the birds merely learn landmarks, applying the senses that we all have, or whether they possess a sixth sense. After the 1890s, science, scholarship, and the pigeon fancy seemed to diverge until the 1960s, when the late William Keeton began doing systematic research on avian navigation at Cornell.

We still don't know exactly how pigeons navigate. What we have learned is some of the things they can perceive. Pigeons, and perhaps all birds, have a sensory palette so broad and deep it can make a mere human feel as though he is deaf, blind, and has lost his senses of taste and smell. For instance, they certainly use the sun as a compass; while we can do this, too, for us it is not a hereditary, instinctual capability. Pigeons have been proven to be able to detect the faint electromagnetic field of the earth. Keeton found that birds carrying bar magnets had trouble homing on overcast days, while birds with pieces of unmagnetized metal that weighed the same were not affected. Pigeons may be able to detect local variations in gravity. Almost all birds can apparently sense changes in the barometer; you may have seen the dramatic arrival of wild migrants as a front approaches, or the increased activity at bird feeders before a blizzard. Pigeons can hear "infrasound," the low-frequency noise made by wind blowing over a mountain range or waves on a rocky shore, over distances of hundreds or even thousands of miles. They see polarized light and colors within ultraviolet. Finally, recent research from Italy shows that, at least in places where the prevailing winds are constant, pigeons can *smell* their way home!

So which of these invisible-to-human senses do they use to navigate? As details of research pile up at Pisa and at the Cornell Laboratory of Ornithology, it seems that perhaps they use all of the above, just as a human might use a map, the sun, and memory. If the sun is obscured by clouds, pigeons will use their magnetic compass, and so on down the line. Although the ability to use these cues is inherent, how the individual bird learns it is important. If a young bird does not spend time outside its loft before its first homing flight, it may never return. And, amazingly, pigeons from different locations apparently rely more on one set of cues than another. While the scientists at Pisa demonstrated that their birds were most dependent on their senses of smell, the Cornell birds apparently ignored smells completely. And now it seems that birds may use entirely different cues to home to lofts one mile apart. The more science shows us of navigation, the more it seems like magic.

 IN THE 1950S EASTON, MASS-achusetts, was a small town, still rural. In most respects it was typical of its time and place, with almost no connections to a Boston only twenty-five miles to the north. But very few small towns have buildings by that grand architect of the Gilded Age, Henry Richardson. His patrons were the Ames family, once feudal lords of Easton and still famed for grand estates, politics, botany, and prize cows. I grew up thinking that every town in America conducted its business in huge, vaguely Pre-Raphaelite edifices of stone and wood, and that every small-town library resembled a medieval cathedral well-stocked with nineteenth-century scientific texts.

I was the first child of two parents who read, and they unself-consciously and probably unintentionally taught me to read before I was four. By the time I was old enough to ride my bike the three miles to the Ames Free Library I had proven my ability to the point where I was allowed full access to the adult stacks. At that age my taste ran to tales of adventure and natural history, or, better yet, books that combined both: *Kon Tiki*, William Beebe's *Pheasant Jungles*, the works of Ernest Thompson Seton. In the adult stacks, way up the right-hand side in tall dim bookcases under the vaulted wood ceiling, was a treasure trove of such stuff, books of the kind that most modern town libraries throw away or at best sell off for ten cents, disfigured by "discontinued" or "deaccessioned" stamps. There were musty volumes on the snakes of Burma and the frogs of Venezuela, encyclopedic monstrosities on tropical fish that weighed as much as a Labrador retriever, and Edwardian poultry tomes with engraved illustrations in half-leather bindings. I ate this stuff up, packing four or five thick books a week home in my bike basket. I devoured Darwin's *Animals and Plants Under Domestication*, George Ryley Scott's *A History of Cockfighting*, Wallace's *Malay Archipelago*, Belt's *Naturalist in Nicaragua*, Tegetmeier's *Pigeons: their Structure, Varieties, Habits, and Management*, learning and retaining scraps of knowledge so esoteric they have never served me for anything but delight.

Unfortunately, I was a nervous, dreamy kid, and I had quite unconsciously developed the odd habit of pinching off the corners of pages as I read and chewing them like gum. For a long time I escaped the notice of the authorities. Then one day my mother hung up the phone with a perplexed face and announced that we were going to see Mrs. Poirier. The "we" put me on notice; I never had needed help to see the head librarian before.

I was always a little afraid of Mrs. Poirier, though

39

she was far from the clichéd library dragoness. A serenely beautiful woman in her seventies who must have weighed all of ninety pounds, she had the disconcerting habit of not quite approving of my choices in literature without going so far as to tell me to put a book back. She radiated a sort of Puritan rectitude I found a lot more intimidating than wrath.

But I really had no idea what I had done until I saw the thick stack of books on her desk, each with its neatly clipped edges. "You are the only person who has taken out all these books. In fact, you are the only person who has taken out some of them in the last twenty years. Do you *enjoy* destroying something that you love enough to check out three times? That is much older than you are?"

I hung my head and could not answer. My mother didn't help matters by beginning to natter on about being sure that I didn't mean any harm, interrupting her defense to demand of me *why* I had torn off the corners.

I was about to cry when Mrs. Poirier miraculously came to my defense. "Stephen, is it possible that you didn't *know* you were doing this?" I nodded. "You realize that if you keep on I can no longer allow you to borrow adult books?" Another nod. "I'll make a list of the ones you have already *damaged.*" I winced at the word. "And until you have proved to me that you have more respect for books than you have shown, you will show me every book when you return it."

"Yes, Mrs. Poirier."

40

"And now we have had enough of that. You have checked out every book in this library that has anything to do with pigeons. I believe I shall introduce you to my friend Mr. Anderson. He has some pigeons that I think you will enjoy."

I never quite understood Mrs. Poirier's motives; still, I will always be thankful for her grace. And, even more so, for her introduction to Mr. Anderson, who was a find and a source, the first artist in fancy pigeons I ever met.

Uncle Joe Derosier was still living, but sinking slowly from the emphysema and heart condition that would kill him. Doctors had forbidden him to keep birds, and in any case he lived forty miles away, an impossible distance for a kid on a bike. And all the other pigeoneers I knew were obsessed homer men who cared only about racing.

I met Mr. Anderson—no amount of concentration will bring back his first name, and he was far more formal than the racers, all of whom I addressed as "Andy" or "Max"—about a week after the library incident, walking in from the street through an arbor of flowers that blazed like a late Impressionist painting. A slender, aged man in wire-rimmed glasses, the male counterpart of Mrs. Poirier, leaned on a hoe at the end of the path, and reached out gravely to shake my hand. He then lead me around the house, past more vivid flower beds than I had ever seen in my life, to his loft, a low, wide structure encrusted with climbing roses. The old gardener beckoned me forward. I stepped over the threshold, blinking in dim light, conscious of the familiar smell, the rustle and coo and flap, but unable to see well.

"Come on forward, son, into the aviary." (I was conscious even then that "aviary" was a word out of books; most of the fliers I knew said "fly pen.") "You can see better, and most of the birds are out there." I walked out into filtered sun and knew I had just taken another irrevocable step. The aviary was full of the most beautiful pigeons I had ever seen, fifty walking, strutting, flying flowers. And I wanted them *all*. *Now*.

Uncle Joe had kept some fancy breeds—the tumblers, a few fantails—but nothing like these. The first birds to catch my eye were, I knew from my reading, Jacobins. They were a kind often pictured, but I had never made sense of the illustrations,

JACOBIN—
white head just peeping out from its mane.

which seemed to be a pigeon topped by a wheel or sunburst of feathers instead of a head; wherever the head was, it was not visible. Now for the first time I understood: "Jacks" grew circular rosettes on both sides of their necks that met fore and aft to form a sort of monk's cowl around their small

42

heads. Some were white and really, rather than metaphorically, resembled flowers; others, more interestingly, were black or rust red with white caps peeping like tonsured heads from their ruffs.

The Jacks sat placidly for the most part, or moved slowly, their ridiculous manes bobbing in the breeze. But the small African owls were as active as my homers. These were tiny aggressive pigeons, not much bigger than doves, with round skulls and short parrot's beaks. They came in rich solid colors—black, sulfur yellow, dun, red, barred blue. Although they weren't as exotic as the Jacobins, they had presence and personality.

The third breed was one I couldn't put a name to. These had smooth black heads and throats, and black tails. Their heads were surrounded by a shell of hard, curly white feathers. All the rest of their feathers were white, including enormous muffs on their legs. They evoked lace, flowers again, feather boas, Victorian ladies' dresses.

"Those are *Schmalkaldener Mohrenkopfs* from Germany. They may be the only ones in the country." Mr. Anderson had noticed my amazement. In addition to the three very fancy breeds, the loft contained many plebian homers and rollers—the last a common flying tumbler. I guessed, correctly, that these were foster parents for the blinkered, dreamy Jacobins, the short-billed owls, the rare Schmalkaldeners.

My sudden *want* at the sight of these apparitions was something new. I had so far been fascinated by what my birds did and how they did it—action, homing, sport, the stimulating anxieties of race day. Now, suddenly, with these old pictures come to life, I was captivated by how they *looked*.

I never had much advice from Mr. Anderson. He was a rather remote ancient, not given to easy conversation with children. I only saw him once or twice after he gave me the birds, and it was possible to get the impression that he was waiting with well-disguised impatience to go back to his flowers and birds. Still, I owe him for the first stirrings of at least two future enthusiams: that of the collector and that of the breeder.

The fancy breeder's impulse is to art, but I had not yet been seized by anything so sophisticated. All animal keeping is a mix of Edward Wilson's "biophilia," of naturalists' curiosity, of, at least when it involves the higher animals, an impulse toward communication and companionship. But for many of us, particularly those who deal with the small, the colorful, the diverse, and the rare, with reptiles and tropical fish and birds, keeping can also involve the collector's lust to possess. I didn't know it, but the *want* that welled up in me at that moment was to be an intermittent, at times controlling, passion that has driven me to exaltation and despair, not just for pigeons, but for old books, old guns, new fly rods, paintings, and more; one that has made me pile up collections, one that has driven me to the financial edge, one that seems to include in it the opposite passion, to pare down my possessions to a spartan few that I can carry as I travel . . .

But all of this came later. I bicycled home to beg my father to let me keep some fancies in my loft, fearing that he found nonracing pigeons effete. He grunted "It's your loft, put anything you want in it," and returned to his paper. I saved my allowance for two more weeks and at the end of this almost unbearable wait went home with a pair of owls—black cock, yellow hen—and two white Jacobins.

I began breeding these birds and a few homers that year. My attitude toward the birds then was pure innocent acquisitiveness; I admired them as beautiful, sentient objects rather than thinking about how to make the fancies into better show birds or the homers into faster fliers. Except for the fascinations of observing behavior—I already was a naturalist and was only beginning to be a collector—I didn't even care if they bred. Which was just as well. While the homers thrived, the Jacks needed to have their feathers trimmed to *see* well enough to mate, and kept coming up with infertile eggs. While the owls were tough and fecund I felt that there was something wrong with using foster feeders and so usually only raised one youngster out of each clutch of two—they spilled enough from the sides of their ridiculous short bills to starve the smaller squab.

Also, I considered my loft a refuge from my father's persistent "culling," a euphemism for sending off the slow fliers to my grandfather's to be made into pigeon pie. I had read my Darwin at the Ames Free Library—his *Variation of Animals and*

Plants under Domestication is a fine early pigeon text—but I had not yet accepted the idea that to improve the breed you must not keep every individual.

When Charles Darwin trained his formidable power of analysis on the domestic pigeon he was already seeking knowledge of why and how life on earth varies. And, of course, the existence of separate breeds meant that breeders had already developed practical methods of selection. Darwin's contribution was to show that various extreme types of "modern" breeds were connected in the historical past. Breeders engaged in perfecting a single kind of pigeon were looking at just a few generations and were too close to their birds to see the larger picture clearly.

He began his work on pigeons by telling why they were ideal subjects for his studies. "I have been led to study domestic pigeons with particular care, because the evidence that all the domestic races are descended from one source is far clearer than with any other anciently domesticated animal . . . And lastly, because . . . the amount of variation has been extraordinarily great."

He was not exaggerating. Only three domestic animals show a comparable range of physical types to the pigeon: the dog, the chicken, and (maybe) the goldfish. The pigeon may well combine more features attractive to the breeder-artist than the other three. It is fecund—four or five broods a year are possible—and has a convenient length of gesta-

46

tion: pigeon eggs hatch in eighteen days, the young fledge five weeks later and are sexually mature themselves at six months. Pigeons can *do* various things, unlike a goldfish or (unless you are a cockfighter) a chicken. If you must cull a pigeon, it will not leave a hole in your heart the way putting down a dog will, and you can eat it, like the chicken. The pigeon's lifestyle enables it to be held in close quarters, and you may even be able to fly it free in the city—try that with a kennel, or a coopful of chickens. You can choose from any number of roles: friend, general of a sky army, athletic trainer, God, genetic sculptor. You can *be* natural selection, with the power to change the looks and even habits of an animal in your lifetime, steal your neighbor's flocks, seduce his hens, even if you are tied to a patch of city rooftop and a demeaning job.

And finally, pigeons are scaled, fortuitously, to the human hand. In 1901 Lewis Wright wrote: ". . . we believe a great deal of the charm of the pigeon fancy lies in the facility with which a bird can be thus held *in the hand* and examined. A fowl cannot be so: and the facility with which pigeons can, as apart from the cumbersome bodies of poultry, and the fragility and wildness of smaller birds, we suspect gives a sense of *personal* possession and enjoyment that counts for so much in the long run."

As Darwin said, these user-friendly birds descended from one wild source, the rock dove. "Real" rock doves, as opposed to their feral relatives descended from escaped strays, live in an area

47

that stretches from the Hebrides through the Indian subcontinent and includes large portions of the Central Asian desert and North Africa. Anyone who has ever looked at a city pigeon would recognize these birds as kin. They have the same flight patterns, the same plump shape and pointed wings. They wheel in flocks around bare cliffs the way the urban birds do around skyscrapers. Most are blue-gray with white rumps and two black bars on each wing, the pattern that fanciers call "blue bar," and one that is common in feral pigeons. They build loose nests on ledges in which they lay two chalky white eggs brooded by the male during the day, and the female at night. The eggs hatch in eighteen days to disclose two tiny, nearly naked, blind, and incredibly ugly babies, among the most helpless of any newborn birds, with huge bills and flimsy necks and nearly transparent yellow skins. For the first few days both parents feed them "pigeon milk," a sort of milky curd formed from the lining of their crops or upper stomachs. After this time they begin to pump them full of grain softened by water. It is a ridiculous procedure. The parent approaches the squeaking, begging young one, who inserts its bill into the corner of the adult's mouth. The adult then flaps, retches, and does leg squats to force up the liquid grain mixture.

In four or five weeks the babies are enormously fat and pretty well covered with feathers. They are now at their greatest lifetime weight and tenderness. This is the time to take them away if you want to eat squab. Shortly thereafter they will lose weight and toughen up as they begin to fly. The males may feed them intermittently for another couple of weeks. The female is already sitting on another clutch of eggs.

On this humble base fanciers have for thousands of years built their breeds, choosing first ability, then color and shape as their impulses took flight. The reasons for some changes are apparent if you study behavior and appearance. Pouters, for instance, especially the primitive Spanish breeds, are caricatures of macho pigeon sexuality. The cocks have more or less permanently inflated crops, heavy skulls, and are constantly and aggressively on the lookout for females. Even the hens are seductive. Here natural and human selection converge; it's not hard to imagine some ancient Arab noticing that the odd pigeon with the large crop was more than usually successful in bringing home mates and therefore breeding from him and his large-cropped descendants in order to increase his collection (or larder). From here the step to sport is almost inevitable.

Other connections of form and function are less clear. Nineteenth-century naturalists thought that the wattle on Bagdads, dragoons, and carriers might be the visible sign of a highly developed sense of smell. Later scientists ridiculed the idea; still, after the Pisa experiments, who can tell? But why is the ability to tumble usually one correlated with pearly white eyes, or the possession of extra tail feathers with a curved, trembling neck? Why

49

do deep bronze neck feathers and their dilute, a pale gold, only exist in two geographically and genetically remote breeds, the Catalonian tumbler and the archangel?

Of course, the reasons behind other forms are more than clear. It's easy to see why "squabbing" breeds have come to resemble small chickens in shape and size, or why pigeons of exceptionally beautiful color and pattern, like Oriental frills or the many German "toy" breeds or the fantail or Mr. Anderson's Schmalkaldeners, would be saved and developed. But whatever their origins, centuries of whim, will, and obsession have given us literally hundreds of breeds, ranging from six ounces to three and a half pounds in weight, birds that fly a thousand miles to home or for twenty-four hours above the loft, birds that can't fly but only turn somersaults each time they leave the ground, birds with wattles and crests and frills and muffs—in fact a pigeon for every fancy.

In the early sixties serious breeding was still beyond me. I just watched and enjoyed my birds. I don't think I ever got a fertile egg out of the Jacobins and developed a mild dislike for the feckless breed. My homers homed, but never in the money; I fancied that my grandfather licked his lips whenever he looked at my little loft. When I left home in 1967 with all the gales of the sixties roaring in my ears, I no longer had time for pigeons. I continued to find them interesting, but pigeons are not fit companions for nomads. During my first brief marriage, at nineteen, I attempted to keep the last pair of Anderson owls in a converted shipping crate perched across two sawhorses in the living room; as a conversation piece, it beat tropical fish. When the marriage collapsed, I sent the birds to the pet store and burned the crates in the fireplace under the star map and the bullet holes where I had tested my brother's 9mm Walther. Pigeons demand at least a semblance of stability; I was for the road.

CHAPTER 5

IT WAS ABOUT THIRTEEN years later when I lifted a beautiful baldhead tumbler out of a cardboard box on Jim Skidmore's kitchen table. In the intervening years I had moved on an average of once a year, and until recently my most lasting companions had been falcons. Hawks, though their possession is bound up in a medieval knot of legal restrictions, suited a nomad's lifestyle. They could hunt their own food, sleep in a square foot of space, accept (if properly introduced) almost any human presence, and both demanded and gave fairness but not loyalty. Sooner or later, they mostly disappeared over the hill; meanwhile, they were lots of fun. But lately, I had to admit that I had settled down. I still had a hawk, but he was a captive-bred baby who regarded me as some un-likely compound of mama, slave, and God, who once after being out overnight stooped to me in such a hysterical rush that he snapped the leather lure off its string. I was monogamous, living with a woman, Betsy Huntington, who was to give us the best years of our lives. I still rented, but I had lived in the battered adobe and its five acres of fruit trees and asparagus for a couple of years. I even pruned the trees. In short, the signs were right when Skidmore, an obsessed falconer, decided to show me his new hawk food.

"Aww, Jim . . . that's too pretty to feed to a hawk. That's a baldhead tumbler."

"Cute, aren't they?" Despite the words he seemed unmoved. I reached in again.

"There's *two*? It looks like a cock and a hen. Do you really need them?"

"Naah. Take 'em home with you." And so I began, or renewed, my adult relationship with pigeons. Never one to do anything by halves—a hint of my father's personality?—I immediately sent off for a subscription to the *American Pigeon Journal,* a very informal magazine that keeps the fancy in tenuous touch. And in its pages I soon found an ad for Catalonian tumblers, an ancient and colorful breed that I had coveted since my childhood but had thought did not exist in America. A letter brought the reply that the fancier was disposing of his stock, that I could have all he had left for fifty dollars.

They arrived by air a week later. Betsy took the wheel for the hundred-mile drive back from Albuquerque while I balanced the unwieldy cardboard box on my knees and peered through the air holes. I was a bird-obsessed child again, and the little I could see told me I would not be disappointed. When we got back I practically ran into the porch to decant the eleven birds into our new loft. They

53

bustled about, drank, and bathed. I just stood there grinning. *"Look* at them. Did you ever see *anything* like that?"

Betsy never shared my obsessiveness but she too was delighted with these birds. I don't know why Catalonians are rare; they are a pigeon to disarm the pigeon-hater, and one so beautiful that, if you are inclined to keep animals, you will covet a pair immediately. Most pigeons, however handsomely marked, are dull-colored, ranging in hue from brown to gray. Some of the Cats were of more or less regulation pigeon color and pattern, though the reds, in most breeds an unremarkable brown, were the brilliant chestnut of an Irish setter. But five of the new arrivals were carbon black, with their entire heads, necks, and breasts the reflective copper of a new penny. I am not speaking metaphorically of normal pigeon iridescence, but of a whole new color, one I had never before seen on pigeons. Several of the others had their entire bodies subtly burnished with deep red bronze. Half of them had white tails on colored bodies. And one of these last might have been the prettiest and most unusually colored pigeon I had ever seen: his body was black, his tail white, and his head and neck were pale yellow-gold with glosses of green and pale purple. All these colors were painted on tight, athletic fliers' bodies—no frills or crests or feathers on the feet here. They had the pearly white tumbler eyes. And they were small, no more than half the size of homers.

Not only were they beautiful, but they could fly,

for hours at a time; fly acrobatically, flipping and flaring and tumbling; fly in mock wars, "capturing" flocks of other pigeons and luring them in through my doors; fly, it was alleged, in "combat" against falcons in the islands off Spain, outvying their fierce competitors nine times out of ten. Remembering my boredom, finally, at my old fancy breeds' do-nothing ways, I was sure that I had found the perfect pigeon.

They really did seem to have everything; their beauty, glimpsed so long ago in blurry black-and-white photos in my father's pigeon books and fulfilled in so much blazing color in the back-porch loft, was only the beginning. In Catalonian tumblers, I began to find, were intellectual and esthetic rewards beyond the beauty of golden neck feathers. In them, in their habits and genes, were encoded the history of peoples as well as pigeon breeds, links with my beloved falcons, challenging sports, even benevolent experiments in modern science. They pulled together my schizoid interests as no other domestic animal ever had.

History? The Cats, as my pigeon-breeder friends called them, are as close to a Neolithic Ur-breed as exists today. You can see elements of all the modern tumblers in their shapes and colors and markings: a "fish" eye here, the bronzing that foreshadows that of the modern marathon-flying (and nontumbling) tippler here, a white tail (shared by more specialized breeds from Eastern Europe and Arabia) there. Nor do they resemble only tumblers. They have rather wide eye ceres—those circles of bare skin around the eyes that, with their white eyes, gave them a perpetually startled look—and these ceres turn red at any exposure to the sun. Such ceres are usually considered characteristic of the Bagdad-Barb (for Barbary) group rather than of tumblers. But some Cats, especially stout black short-beaked males, look uncannily like small delicate Barbs. Others sport frills, rows of reversed feathers along the fronts of their necks, like "owls"; or feathered feet; or high-set tails and low-held wings, like Oriental rollers or primitive fantails. All are recognizable as Catalonians, but they are incredibly diverse, as though a hundred shadowy breeds lurk just below the surface.

Doubtless they *did*. Spain, as anyone knows, preserves many old habits, customs, and objects, and had, at least until now, preserved an ancient Moorish or Arab pigeon that had later dispersed through Europe and the Middle East, turning into other breeds through man's hothouse evolutionary selection. (Ironically, a friend, a pigeon man and scholar from Spain, tells me that the Catalonian, as well as the ancient Spanish pouter breeds that would be my next project, are almost extinct in Spain, a victim of the standardization sweeping the world. It's a little unsettling to think that the last two flocks of this ancient breed may be in Magdalena, New Mexico, and on the Alamo Navajo Reservation.)

You could say that the Catalonian's ancient, primitive, unspecialized characteristics confirm Spain's isolation from the modern world. Spain also practices three flying sports, two of which are unique and all of which can be traced by lore and a tenuous paper trail at least as far back as Moorish Spain and thence by inference to the beginning of pigeon (and human urban) culture.

In those early cities, just as in today's, falcons must have harassed the wheeling flocks of rock doves or semidomesticated manure pigeons. Although we moderns simplistically divide the world into hawks and doves, pigeons are far from easy victims; falconers know that when hawk goes against pigeon it is usually the prey that outflies the predator and lives to test the falcon's skill on another day.

An early city dweller with the leisure to hide and watch would also see one pigeon flock pull on another with magnetic attraction until they coalesced like a splitting amoeba in reverse, then return to their home roost with their followers. Finally, observing even more closely, the same watcher might see a strutting cock from one utilitarian dovecote inflate his crop and display, even exaggerate, his charms, harassing the hen of his choice until she surrendered and allowed herself to be seduced back to his home. As humans are anthropomorphic, biophilic (*biophilia* is scientist-writer Edward Wilson's word for the innate fascination with other life on earth), and, above all, playful, the foregoing three simple facets of pigeon behavior gave rise to three ancient sports.

I have never been able to find more than a couple of one-sentence mentions of the most exotic of the flying sports: *Arruixada*, the pigeon-versus-falcon competition of the Balearics; I don't even know if the falcons were trained, or whether the pigeons were sent up against wild local birds that nested in the cliffs above the towns. Contests of animal against animal are common in most old cultures, who sometimes seem more realistic in their acceptance of death than do most modern ones. This one was fairer than most, and pretty benign; the falcon was of course immune to hurt, and, if the clandestine "pigeon derbies" practiced by a few American falconers today are any indication, the pigeon probably escaped without being touched nine times out of ten. The modern version uses straightforward racing homers. The bird of choice in Majorca was the escampadissa roller, a Catalonian-style tumbler and slip-slider that was probably even *harder* for the hawk to catch. Its name comes from the Spanish verb *escampar*, used colloquially in Majorca to mean disperse, or scatter.

Whether one approves of it or not, *Arruixada* seems to have vanished into the foggy regions where the former pastimes of mostly oral cultures go when no one records them. The other two sports are very much alive.

In terms of sheer numbers, the most popular pigeon sport today is probably modern Belgian-style racing. But its apparatus and level of organization make it a sport for the relatively affluent. Therefore, the widest-spread sky competition is what Brooklyn fanciers still call *La Guerra*. In New York, Barcelona, Modena, Damascus, and Beijing, flocks of pigeons are sent up against "enemy"

58

AMERICAN DOMESTIC
FLIGHT—
Brooklyn's rooftop warrior.

flocks. The fanciers try to maneuver the birds together into one mass, then signal their own
pigeons to come home. If the birds respond
promptly and "crash" to the rooftop they will most
likely drag the other fanciers' kits down too. Now
the winner can catch the strays, usually with the
aid of a long-handled net (known in New York as a
"hoople"). This is the kind of pigeon-flying cele-
brated in *On the Waterfront*.

In Wendell Levi's incredible monograph *The
Pigeon*, he says that references exist in the Talmud
barring "flyers of pigeons" from bearing witness
because they are gamblers who steal one another's
pigeons—another piece of evidence both of pigeon
flying's antiquity and its Middle Eastern origins. By
1327 the city of Modena in Italy had codified the
conditions under which you returned (or did not
return) your acquisitions. Under *di buona amicizia*
you returned them to their owner free of charge;
the game was the thing. *Di buona guerra* meant that
you sold them back under a price agreed upon be-
forehand. Under *a guerra dichiarata* you had no obli-
gation to return them. And with *a guerra ad ultimo*

sangre you killed the captured pigeon and hung it from the loft in full view of your enemy.

New York writer Jack Kligerman, who has described Brooklyn's fliers in his fine book *A Fancy for Pigeons*, says that the modern sky warriors have virtually the same terms: "free catch," "exchange," "catch-keep," and "catch-kill." Kligerman also tells of the ultimate revenge of the ancient Italian Triganini: They would attach a powerful firecracker-like glass bottle to a captured bird, wait for the enemy to fly his birds, then send up the flying bomb to blow the whole flock out of the sky.

I had hopes of, someday, spreading the Catalonians among my local friends so that we could fly *di buona amicizia* against each other. But first, we needed birds. I knew nothing of the Catalonian's worldwide status, but I knew I was one of maybe two or three fanciers in North America to have *any* . . . and I had only about fifteen. The "serious" breeding that I had avoided when I was young seemed the only way to realize my sudden objectives: to multiply my numbers; to save the old breed (for new regulations had made importing new blood from Spain a frightfully expensive bureaucratic nightmare); to, if possible, increase the number of the rarer-colored birds and uncover "new" recessive colors hidden in these birds' genes; to eliminate some dubious-looking characteristics in a few of my birds that made me suspect that some had been crossed with modern rollers; and to do the last without inbreeding so much that

60

I would weaken my birds, no easy task with so few to start with.

Pigeon genetics—"pigeon science," as writer and pigeon naturalist Shannon Hiatt calls it—is a surprisingly well-studied branch of biology. One reason for this is probably that of Lewis Wright: the user-friendliness of the pigeon. Another is, of course, the range of variation available. And yet another big one is that a few dedicated geneticists have been pigeon fanciers, especially Willard F. "Doc" Hollander. Doc, who is retired these days, is an unusual combination of pigeon maniac, inspired teacher, indefatigable correspondent, and innovative scientist. He still collects and breeds strange pigeons and shares his knowledge of them with like-minded cronies around the country, a group into which I had unwittingly tapped. I found that there was a vast literature on inheritance of specific traits and colors. But with the Cats I was out on the edges of serious research; some Catalonian colors were so odd that American breeders, even the scientists among them, didn't even have names for them, never mind genetic charts. What on earth is a color that translates as "little rat," a slightly iridescent silver-gray flecked all over with black?*

I called Dan Konen, who sold them to me, to ask his advice on breeding, and he laughed. "Mix and match," he said, "and you'll get a surprise in every

---

*This bird, incidentally, died before it could reproduce. His parents, brothers, and sisters, bred in fantastic combinations, have never produced another like him.

nest." He added a little advice on uncovering recessive traits, and I was on my own.

I had been looking at photos of Catalonians for years and had a pretty good idea of what I wanted, a Platonic ideal of *the* Catalonian tumbler. All breeders of domestic animals (and, I'm sure, plants) have such a template, sometimes purely in the mind, sometimes codified onto a standard or detailed description. A standard will include an idealized picture and assign numerical values to various physical characters, adding up to a perfect, never-attained one hundred points. To have a standard, though, you must have a group of dedicated breeders; with this breed, I was on my own.

Still, the best of my birds, the ones that were simultaneously less like familiar English-type tumblers and more like one another, shared enough characteristics to give me a clue. They were *very* small, smaller than any breed I had ever owned, stout, compact, and hard-feathered. They had rather square heads, like the old "depressed-brain" homer of my youth, and stout, short conical bills. They had broad eye ceres and pearl eyes. Several had frills, and all these birds were at least brushed with bronze. Some looked like their iron black plumage was just starting to rust; some were brilliant metallic bronze with green highlights; one, as mentioned, was gold. Even the reds seemed to owe the unusual brilliance of their color to a touch of bronze.

Not all my new birds shared these traits, although every one had at least a couple. There was a hen who was richly bronzed but had the long thin bill, high forehead, skinny cere, and dark eyes of a roller—or a rock dove. There was a beautiful blue cock with a white tail that had almost everything but bronzing—except that he was huge, almost as big as a homer. And there was a sulfur yellow hen that might have been perfect but for her orange eyes. Still, it was a start.

My first matings were more or less random, though I did attempt to make up several pairs of "pure"-type Cats. The first generation of young came out in an astounding rainbow of colors, but with many odd types: large ones, long skinny ones, a crested bird, and one with his breast and neck feathers all curled like a so-called "Chinese" owl. Since the Chinese owl is actually descended from a Spanish bird known as a *chorrera* or Spanish frill, I took the appearance of this trait as more evidence of the Catalonian's relation to *everything*.

I didn't even consider culling any of the first generation. Recessive genetic traits were already appearing; that is, traits that were invisible beneath the dominant characteristics of the parent birds but, when carried by both parents, manifest in the young. But now, to *really* fan the cards in the genetic deck, I would have to inbreed—mate brother to sister—or linebreed—mate father to daughter, mother to son. Such practices do not weaken the offspring if not carried out too far; they can be necessary to fix desired traits as well as to expose hidden recessive colors. The process takes a lot of time, though, even in such swift-maturing creatures as pigeons. Besides, pigeons, though not as fiercely monogamous as birds of prey or geese, remain attached to old mates; divorce and remarriage can be tedious.

And delightful. I found a new pleasure: waiting for the babies to feather out to see if their color was something longed for, predicted out of Quinn's genetic textbook or combined from the parents, or, maybe better still, something entirely new, always a possibility with Catalonians. Betsy and I would lift the furious mother birds, ignoring their pecks and grunts and the buffeting of their wings, to see if any color had sprouted yet from the porcupine quills of the new feathers. By our second season we had blue, black, silver and dun, recessive red, dominant or "ash" red, bronze, combinations of the last three, yellow, "De Roy" (a color for which there were no genetic charts but that was described in the nineteenth century), almond, and gold. For patterns we had splash, white-tailed, white-lighted, beard, baldhead, and mottle. And there were several birds we could only describe, not name.

Except for bronze, which seemed to over- or underlay most everything in the breed, the "good" colors remained elusive. Recessives weren't hard to breed—you just mated one to its equivalent, if you had one, or to a relative, if you didn't. But "dilutes," including the incredible gold, were another story. Dilute colors are simple recessive versions of so-called intense colors, with fewer pigment granules. But baby dilutes tended to be oddly delicate until their first molt, and we lost as many as we saved. We really wanted a gold-necked silver, but since such a pigeon is a double dilute (of a bronze-necked blue or black) we never managed to breed one. I haven't to this day.

And to make matters more complicated, we were producing a lot of pigeons. Our loft at that time was within an enclosed porch, reached, for some insane architectural whim of our landlady's, through the bathroom. You could sit on the throne and watch the pageant of multicolored pigeons through a screen door, which amused some guests and appalled others. It was all fun—but even I was beginning to admit that there were too many.

Now I am a hunter and a fairly unsentimental naturalist who often kills things and eats them. But to kill such things as these friendly, beautiful, *cute*, little birds just because we had too many of a color—the copper-necked blacks, among the most elegant and characteristic of Catalonians and a color that seemed linked with all the proper physical traits of short beak, large cere, white eye and so forth, bred like fruit flies—seemed heartless in the extreme. I knew it was not immoral, at least by my Darwinian standards, to cull; I just didn't want to.

At which point Rudy Lucero entered our lives, stopping me in the Magdalena "super" market, Trail's End, to enquire about pigeons. Rudy is tall, thin, and dark, quiet, almost scholarly, a little younger than I am. He spoke of how he had kept pigeons off and on since he was a child and wanted to get into some "good" ones, rather than the mongrel tumblers and "feather-foots" common around the village. It seemed I had found my first partner and, I hoped, future competition.

Rudy was no young kid, grateful for any trash bird, but a serious fancier. I gave him as many pairs of those good black-and-bronze surplus birds as I could force on him, plus a lot of the splash or piebald-pattern birds that, although they were perfectly good specimens, didn't appeal esthetically to me. I introduced him to a couple of Albuquerque fanciers I had met, told him a little of my theories about what made a good Catalonian, showed him the *Pigeon Journal.*

And then had to stand aside as he took off. I am perpetually divided, chasing writing, hunting, falconry, old books and guns, training dogs, collecting insects, fishing for trout and catfish, spending my limited money on everything from music to travel to cooking utensils. Rudy was *focused*. A year after he started, he owned two-hundred-odd birds in twenty breeds, was winning shows with his Chinese owls, and had bred colors from the Cats that I had never seen and coveted lustfully. Not that he was ever selfish—he would let me take and breed from any bird that caught my eye. But he did make me, with more than twenty-five years experience, feel a little amateurish. (Years later, long after he had moved close to his wife's family on the Alamo Navajo reservation, I took Shannon Hiatt up to the loft. Shannon is a writer, teacher, and naturalist who may be the most intellectual and scholarly fancier I have ever met. He spent an hour going over the loft and then told me, wonderingly, that "this may be one of the two or three best rare-color and rare-breed lofts in the country.")

By the time we had reached that point, of course, we both had the culling problem again. But by then we had eliminated most of the traits that were undesirable, so real fanciers actually wanted our surplus. And for the others, apart from pigeon pie, we discovered what many other breeders knew before us: kids *love* pigeons, and don't particularly care about quality. We had become mentors.

Early in the fall of 1986 Betsy was diagnosed as having inoperable lung cancer. Brave and merry to the end, she died in November. I could not stay and look through the same windows, so I decided to take a year in New England. I was back in the middle of the nomad-settler paradox at the age of thirty-six; the dogs and the hawk could live out of the truck, but the pigeons couldn't. Reluctantly, I packed up the birds, lofts and all, and brought them to Rudy's at the Alamo reservation. I was on the road again—to Boston, to New Hampshire, finally for six months to a falconer's farm in Maine, where homesickness would drive me back to Magdalena.

But the uncertainties did not make me drop pigeons; when the virus invades an adult, it is harder to shake. Just as I was leaving I got a letter from a Spanish fancier, José Morales, with whom I had started a correspondence a few years back. José, "Pepé" to his friends, had taken a master's degree in English at the University of New Mexico. His note was to tell me that he was coming back to study for his Ph.D. I didn't know it, but Pepé's fascinations were about to introduce me to the strangest of the Spanish sports, and a new chapter in my life with birds.

CHAPTER 6

SPANISH POUTERS, LIKE CAT-
alonians, had always
caught my attention in the
pigeon books. They were
not pretty, not at all con-
ventionally appealing, but
an odd mixture of hand-
some and grotesque. Bull-headed, powerful-look-
ing, wattled, and severe, they seemed the essence
of pigeon masculinity. They had deep hanging
crops, thick legs, and almost ferocious faces; they
had character rather than beauty. They were also,
the books said, as ancient as any breed that existed
and sometimes used as seductive thieves to woo
others' hens home. Their most modern variety, a
slightly more conventional bird bred by crossing
the old breeds to—what else?—Belgian racing
homers, was even known as a *ladron*, or thief. This
was a perfectly pragmatic modern interpretation,
but I found a Portuguese writer's objections delightful: "We don't know why these birds are called
thieves among us, for it is an injustice to call thief
to a little bird, that, at most, conquers, woos, se-
duces, abducts, but does not steal. Conquistador,
yes, that is the word that properly applies to him,
being that he is an untiring and incorrigible lover."

I knew that there were islands of Spanish pigeon culture in the Americas—in Argentina, Mexico City, at least in the past in Cuba, and in Florida, so when I moved to New Mexico I kept my eyes and ears open, and, of course, talked about the breeds to Rudy. He came back from a show in Albuquerque one day with a box that he opened to disclose something I had only dreamed about.

"I thought you might like these. When I saw them for sale, I remembered you talking about them . . ." They were not spectacularly strange birds, but they could be nothing but "Spanish pouters," the broad generic name under which they were sold to Rudy. The cock was more distinctive, with a large globe and a stout wattled head. The hen resembled a short, rotund racing pigeon but with a shorter beak—her crop was barely enlarged. He looked most like the *jerezano* in the books, whereas she resembled the picture of the ladron. I asked him who had sold them, but he hadn't gotten an address. "Some Spanish guy"— he meant New Mexican Spanish—"from Roy." Since Roy is even more isolated than Magdalena, lost in the high plains five hours away—and since Rudy didn't have the man's name—I figured their origins must remain a mystery for now.

Name-brand or not, the new pair captivated me. The cock, in particular, lived up to his breed's reputation; he did almost nothing but chase hens, even leaping off his eggs to chase any attractive female that approached within three feet of the nest. He and his mate raised three young before a

70

sudden crop infection (something I was to find is the bane of pouters, which more than any other breed need moderate, regular, high-quality food) killed the hen. Luckily, two of the young were hens, and, even better for my love of the exotic, they appeared to look more like their large-cropped father than their nondescript mother.

And then Betsy started coughing. Despite Pepé's note, in the next eight months I didn't give Spanish pouters much thought. Once I was back home in Magdalena, though, one of my first actions after getting settled was to call on Pepé in Albuquerque's Valley neighborhood.

Although well within the city limits, much of the Rio Grande Valley still resembles, in the best way, a rural village. The houses are adobe, surrounded by adobe walls and old trees; some of the roads are dead-end, gravel-finished, and puddled; the entire area is laced with *acequias* (irrigation ditches), and livestock, from chickens to horses, is common. Pepé lived in one of the most attractive of these urban villages, on a dead-end street that terminated at a church, in a house and compound that I still covet. He had a huge yard, partially walled and fenced into corrals out back, which enclosed his house and that of his mother-in-law. His own house had a porch overhung by shade trees, a cool place to take your coffee and drinks, even in June—New Mexico's hottest month—plus a raked driveway and flower beds.

And perched on the gabled tin roof above, strutting in the raked gravel of the courtyard, were

71

twins to my old grizzled pouter cock. As I watched from outside the gate, two common pigeons stroked by overhead. The cock on the roof sprang into action and cut up from below like a hungry goshawk but as he pressed in on the tail of his "prey," I sensed that he was not driven by aggression, never mind hunger. I say I sensed it, though of course I knew about it in theory, because never in my life had I seen a bird so sex-mad as to chase passing strays like a hawk.

As I watched them out of sight a tall slender man of my own age emerged from the shade of the porch. He had a long serious scholarly face out of El Greco, thinning hair, and a welcoming grin. "You are Steve. Come in and have some coffee. That's a good bird there, a New Mexican bird— perhaps a relative of yours."

And so we began the routines that would shape the next phase of my life with pigeons. I would soon find that in Pepé Morales I had found a partner to match my own intensity, fascination with history, and scholarly bent, and who far surpassed me in knowledge. Soon he would be spreading out Xerox copies of twelfth-century Spanish translations from the Arabic that spoke of something very like La Suelta, the sport of thieving, translating impatiently into English as I stumbled along behind. But for now I knew he served good black coffee, had a collection of Spanish pigeon articles, photos of all the "real" old ram-headed breeds, many of which he had owned in Spain, and that, like me, he had grown up molded by the tales of the old pigeon men.

And what's more, he wrote—well. On our first visit he gave me a copy of a long narrative poem in English, called *One More Pigeon Story,* that for the first time gave me the feel, the sights, almost the smell of a traditional village pigeon culture.

Pepé's pigeon villages were poor places, "anarchist ground by tradition and necessity/ a tumultuous ocean of the destitute and desperate/ where still a few bandits and a few honest men/ carry sharp vicious knives in their pockets." He goes on to tell how "winter usually hits hard here/ and tightens steel clutches around any man's neck/ especially if he is but an unskilled worker/ who depends for his sustenance on odds and ends/ such as the selling of burned wheat/ the scrounging for second-hand poultry cages/ the betting at a cock fight . . ." And yet, here in this hard place, a hard man like Antonio the goatherd, famed for his "whoremonger's habits/ as well as his drinking/ and his beautiful excellent Laudino Sevillano pigeons," can comment "on the curvature of a smooth head/ the caramel color of a beak/ and the rich cherry glint/ of a perfect eye."

His portrait of villagers who still flew pigeons the way their ancestors did appealed to me on two levels. The simplest one was that birds like these could fit into my current life in Magdalena, in a rural neighborhood not unlike Pepé's, better than either homers or Catalonians (and more actively than any pure fancy breed). Even if you didn't have any neighbors to compete against, you could let your males fly free and they would toll wild pigeons. Any doubt about this could be dispelled

73

in an hour by watching "Loco," the New Mexican cock that had taken off in pursuit of the two wanderers as I arrived that first time. Because Pepé would climb up to the nests under the rafters every evening to remove Loco's current mate to a ground-level loft reserved for surplus birds and foster parents for the careless pouters, he was likely to be courting a new partner every day.

But the other level of fascination, if more intellectual, was even deeper, a unique glimpse into a complex historical-social ecology. I soon came to think of the thief pouter breeders as the last remnants of traditional pre-Industrial-Revolution pigeon culture left in Europe. The Spaniards had never mixed their breeds with other countries, perhaps because they rarely left their native ground, so their pigeons were the last representatives of ancient types.

And, like so many things in the twentieth century, they were almost gone. During the Spanish civil war, soldiers were ordered to confiscate all the pigeons in rebellious areas lest they be used to carry messages. (Spanish pouters are, obviously, good homers as well.) Some breeds became virtually extinct during this time, although Pepé remembers tales of prize birds hidden in boxes under the bed. But the real threat to the old breeds took place after the war, as the new *Palomas Deportivas*, streamlined by crosses with racing homers and rock doves, became the bird of choice for sportsmen. Not only were they more reliable breeders than the ponderous, sex-obsessed* *Laudinos* and

*Which sounds like a contradiction, but the old breeds rarely stopped their pursuit long enough to raise a family.

74

Valencianos, but the government actually promoted and subsidized them.

In 1977, a group of fanciers from Seville, Pepé's home city, formed a club called *La Giralda,* after a famous tower in the cathedral there. Its quixotic purpose, an eleventh-hour rescue of the old breeds, succeeded to the extent that the fanciers and their birds were accepted into the official *Federacion Espanola de Colombicultura.* It seemed that the oldest and oddest pigeons around had been saved by the bell. But that didn't solve my immediate problem: How on earth could I get some?

These days, a harrowing maze of federal regulations covers all international movements of birds and animals. While these rules may be necessary in some cases, they can be frustrating to the honest animal breeder, especially if he is poor. The rule that affects pigeon importation originated in the Newcastle-disease scare of the late 1960s, was prompted by the fears of commercial poultry growers, and states that all imported birds must go into quarantine for ninety days at one of three designated ports of entry, and that if any bird in a given shipment falls ill, all must be destroyed. The fees are set by the government. What it boils down to is that each bird costs over a hundred dollars (over the price you pay to the breeder), and that you get no refund if it dies, nor any guarantee that it will live.

I liked my mongrel "New Mexican pouters," as we had come to call them, just fine as far as their habits went, but they were not spectacular looking. Pepé felt that the mysterious breeder in Roy had

75

"NEW MEXICAN" THIEF POUTER.
Probably a blend of breeds—see the Marchenero and Valenciano. This drawing is based on my old "grizzle" male.

kept both jerezanos and modern pouters. He had, word of mouth had it, died several years ago and his heirs had let the bloodlines mingle. Some birds were stout and big-cropped, but others hardly differed from chunky homers, or even commons.

Probably I would eventually have gone to Spain when Pepé returned—I still plan to—and found some way of bringing back a few birds. But fate intervened in the form of Steve Klein, an Oregonian who had become as obsessed with the Spanish birds as we had. He had bought a few old-style Valencianos from a California fancier, Frank Barrachina, then brought in some show or "Dutch" Valencians from a Dutch breeder in Vancouver. Finally, he had obtained from somewhere one of the strangest of all pigeons, the lobster-tailed balloon-like Marchenero. He had been breeding for a few years and now wanted both to share the wealth and get himself some room. Needless to say, Pepé and I were eager, especially when Klein said he'd send them for the price of their transport.

And so once again I got to see a long-anticipated

dream bird—or, rather, dream *birds*—in the flesh. By the time I got to Albuquerque, three days after they had arrived, Pepé already had two Marcheneros aloft. And they were both working on hens.

They were no more persistent than the New Mexican birds, but their flight style was unique. In addition to enormous globular crops they had long, soft, rounded wings like a hunting owl's. I had thought that their short stiff "tile tails," held down against the ground in all the photos of sitting birds I had seen, would be held forward under the flying bird's body like some sort of brake or spoiler, but instead it splayed out, making the closest approach a pigeon's tail could to that of a kite or swallow. They flew in slow circles with ponderous grace, as though they were aware of the spectacle they were making. And both already had hens in tow.

Pepé then brought me to his individual breeding coops. Not the least appealing virtue of almost all pouters is their tameness—you can keep them in large nestboxes and let them out within days after you acquire them. As long as you treat them well, and advance cautiously, they will settle down and return as though they had lived with you all their lives.

The pairs in the boxes were even better than the Marcheneros. The cock was gorgeously grotesque—grizzled gray with a white head, coarse wattles, fiery eyes, and a crop that brushed the ground—the hen rounded and elegant in white plumage flecked with black. When Pepé let them out she flew to the ground and began to peck. He followed, clapping his wings, and began to rush at her like a fighting bull charging the matador. His tail dragged stiffly, his crop rippled. As he reached her he'd tower up, on his tiptoes, gobbling air, crowing, seeming to dance. She'd peck demurely and edge away. He'd turn and charge again. It was ridiculous and yet, because of the cock's fire, oddly impressive.

He opened the door of another coop where a black hen with white head splashes was sitting tight. "She laid her first egg the night she got here." He removed the cock, who was all black, and tossed him into the fray. He began to court the hen in the driveway too. His crop was much less developed, his technique less intense, but when she skipped up to the roof he followed, flying wing-to-wing with his rival. After a moment she descended and scuttled for her nestbox. Pepé scooped up the black male as he pressed in and held him up to me. "See? He's what the Dutch fanciers have done with the Valenciano in the last few years. Not as much crop; maybe less instinct to seduce the hens. But a prettier head." The black cock had a perfect Roman-nosed curve of skull and beak.

"Maybe we can cross them together," I began, and we went in for coffee and strategy and Spanish brandy.

And here I am, almost up to the present, for the Valencianos are one of my two current breeds. The others, short-faced homers developed for rural

VALENCIANO—
an old male. These are absurdly macho birds. Notice the hanging "beer belly" crop, unlike the high round ones of the New Mexican or Marchenero Pouters.

communications by Dan Konen, are more of a reversion to my roots than any kind of progression and would require another tangent—or maybe another book. But at present, Valencianos are a favorite because they seem to do it all. They are clowns, sexual acrobats, friendly to humans, and appealingly ugly. They can home, probably quite long distances—they'll voluntarily fly the two miles to the village in pursuit of hens and return in an hour. They also fly soaring overhead, displaying; with their raptorial breadth of wing they are quite spectacular, and despite their ponderousness they seem to be in no more danger from hawks than the Cats were. Of course, the huge shimmering flocks of Cats were probably irresistible beacons.

But the Cats, despite their great beauty, were basically all the same but for color. "I liked it better," said Betsy, "when we had fewer than twenty. Now its just a big aquarium." The pouters, slow breeders, individuals, never become so anonymous. They fight, have adulterous relationships, eat from your hand, and bring home strays. They tend to have names. They are, if you are constructed that way—I'm not—quite practical as well. They're big enough to eat. And unsentimental Pepé—who says the Spanish are romantic?—used to remind me that most of the hens his wandering males brought home ended up in pies and stews.

They are less abstract than homers. They perform their sporting roles within sight, on rooftops and in gravel yards, not even at the binocular distances more common for *La Guerra's* feathered warriors. They are interesting to look at, like a bulldog or a lion goldfish. Prettiness is overrated—Valencianos have *character*. The crosses between the angular, excessive Spanish types and the compact, perfect-profiled Dutch have spawned an amazing array of types and colors, so that like a show breeder, or evolution itself, I'm working toward something that I can't quite see yet, looking forward eagerly to each deal of the cards.

Pepé, brought up in *La Suelta*, says that the particular lure of the pouters is sex, period. Certainly they evolved, were selected, as sexually hypertrophic beings. I balk at stating *what* a male human equivalent of a displaying Valencian would be. But certainly there's an element of—I hope at least half-humorous—identification with these priapic birds.

CHAPTER 7

WHEN I WAS A CHILD, I loved pigeons with an uncomplicated and unselfconscious love. In that labyrinth of preconscious choices that can point the way to a life's passion, direction, even work, pigeons and their owners played one of the two or three determining roles. With a few other birds—none as important—and with an assortment of reptiles and amphibians, they fed my biophilia and animal-keeping inclinations to the point where I almost became a zoologist and still write more often about animals than any other subject. Figuring out their tracks in the sky first exercised my scientific imagination as I tried to figure out ways to get inside their senses and to test my hypotheses. And even better, they linked science and the romance of journeying, so that I could never find biology abstract or dessicated.

They were my first door into the joys of sport, of its precision, passion, and intricacies of lore. I never played ball, and hunting and fishing came later, perhaps never would have come without my already-developed love of animals, games, and lore. Subtly, they influenced the way I would spend at least some of my hours for the rest of my life, in collecting and in breeding animals—not just pigeons but dogs, fish, snakes, hawks, and more.

But perhaps the subtlest of all their influences on me, and the most important, was that of the old men, telling stories in the long hours of the summer evening. I can close my eyes and hear the voices: Andy's deep roar, Max's Prussian snap, John Derosier's cough after each gentle pronouncement. I can hear Tim O'Connell's rasping brogue, chased by two fingers of whiskey in a water glass. The stories make rings like rocks dropped in still water, spreading away from the subject of pigeons to almost anything: gambling, baseball, bird dogs, County Cork, fly fishing, wives and their attitudes. And a child sits, hearing words, wisdom, folly; hearing the accents of a dozen countries and ethnicities—Sicilian, Jewish, Polish, Irish; learning all of Boston's clannish neighborhoods; watching cities, countries, worlds opening up.

It was not a bad beginning for someone who was to become a teller of tales, in bars and in books. Ironically, it was also what drove me away from the birds for a while in that excess of snobbery that seems to drive certain adolescents to deny or ignore or flee everything about their roots. I came to think of pigeon-flying as some roguishly shameful lower-class interest. In my first years on my own I avoided pigeon men even when I kept pigeons. Falcons seemed more safely romantic.

But the infection was deep and never cured. As I came back to pigeons, as mature as friends suspect

I will ever be, I found that I could trace their influences through my life, both back and now forward. They fit my present preoccupations—I began to collect the old pigeon books that I had read, to cook squab using French and Italian and Chinese cookbooks. I could use them, without harming them, to train my hawks and bird dogs.

But these were mere sidelines. They lead me into research into the old Mediterranean cultures that form half my own background, one I now acknowledge with pleasure. They gave me insights into language and history. They led me back to Darwin's *Variation*, which I bought and reread for the first time in twenty-odd years, and let me be a genetic sculptor, a breeder, one of that race of maniac who lifts up sitting mother birds three times a day to see if the babies have feathers yet. They gave me a new link to my father, who kept saying, as I showed him these pages, "How the *hell* do you remember that?"

And they sure look appropriate as they wheel above a mud-walled town in the high-desert sky. Pigeon-flying has revealed itself to my slightly more adult mind as a true sport, as rich in tradition and even more multifaceted than falconry. My first animals—my "perennial retainers" as Konrad Lorenz called his jackdaws—pigeons continue to stoke the fires of my fascination with life on earth in all its diversity, the incredible multiplicity of its adaptations, its relations with humans, its myriad ways.

It's evening now; I think I'll go out to the walled yard and see what my family is up to. A pat suffices for the dogs in the doorway, a glance confirms the hawk safe on his perch under the elm, beside the grape arbor. But the pigeons—I have about twenty-five now—have more freedom, and, at dusk, amid the turbulent clouds of the monsoons, I can worry.

I hear a few young squeakers piping from the nests, can see a couple of adolescents preening by the feed trays. A little pack of short-faced homers zips by on an aerial racetrack, though nothing pursues. Two pouters pay court to an indifferent young homer. It is too young to even know what sex *it* is.

Down toward the village, two miles away and a few hundred feet below, I see wings. It's one of the older Vals, returning. In a minute he pitches up to the roof to join the group serenading the youngster. The homers still zip around in circles. A single sunbeam pierces the clouds to tint them red-gold. I drag my coffee can through the feed barrel to fill it and began to shake it, whistling, calling in my birds the way I have since I was eight.

The pigeons are flying.

Magdalena, N.M.
1986–1989

And in the isolation of the sky,
At evening, casual flocks of pigeons make
Ambiguous undulations as they sink
Downward to darkness, on extended wings.

"Sunday Morning," Wallace Stevens